CARWASH ART

Carwash Art

If He Can Charge $500,000, Then Why Can't I Charge $15.95 For Mine and You Can Keep the Book?

Dominic Santora

Dave Bussard

Hard Knocks Publishing

First Printing, 2021

The Deep Blue Skies Towards Money

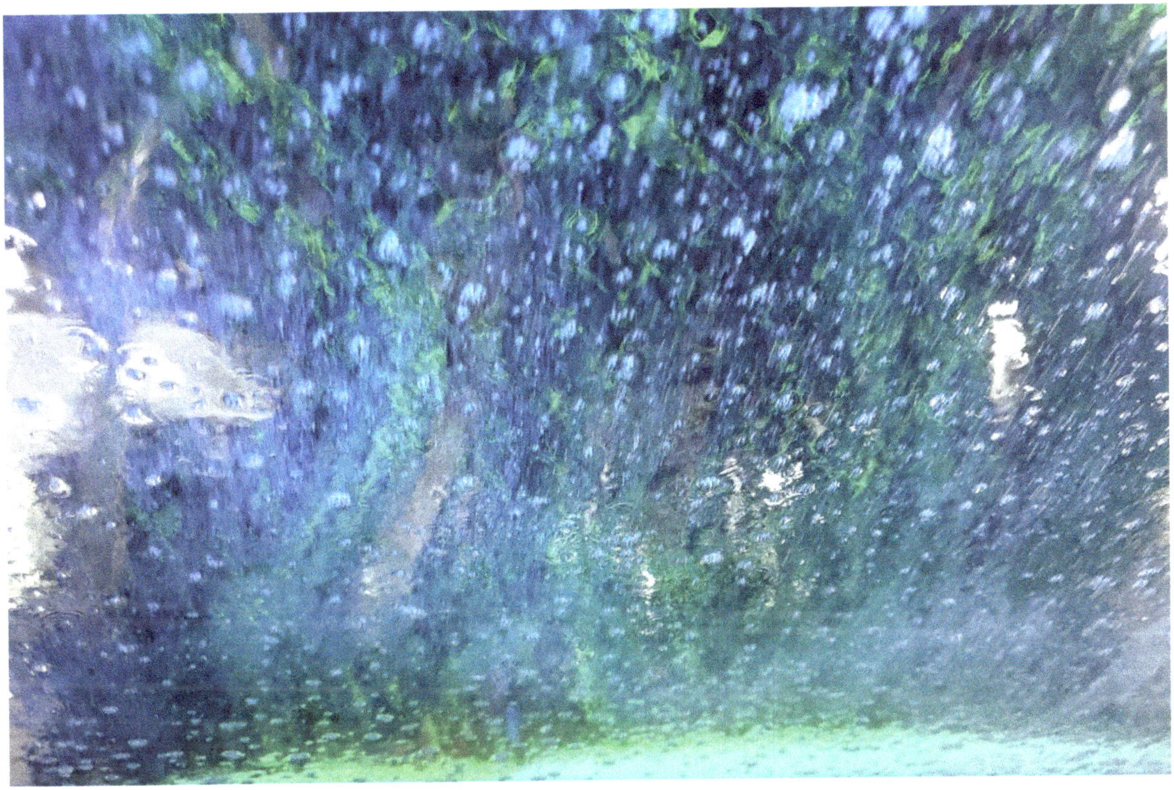

The Big Guy Behind Transparency

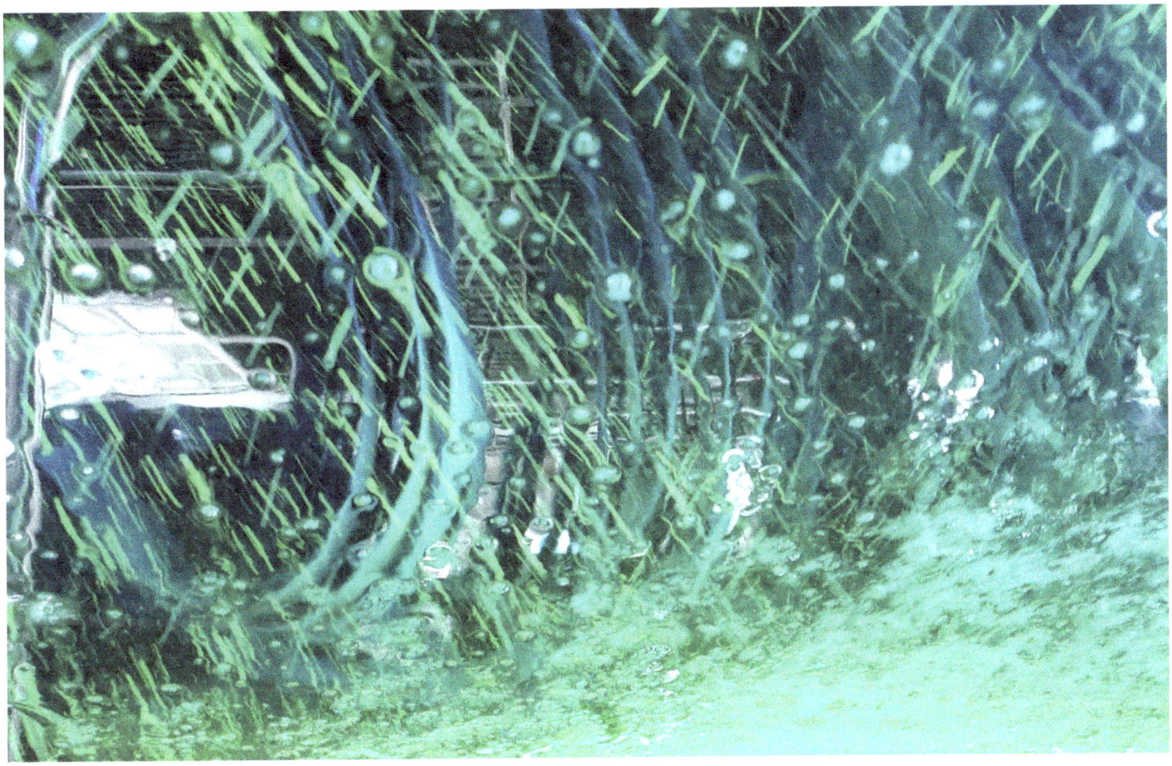

My Computer as It Computes the Deals

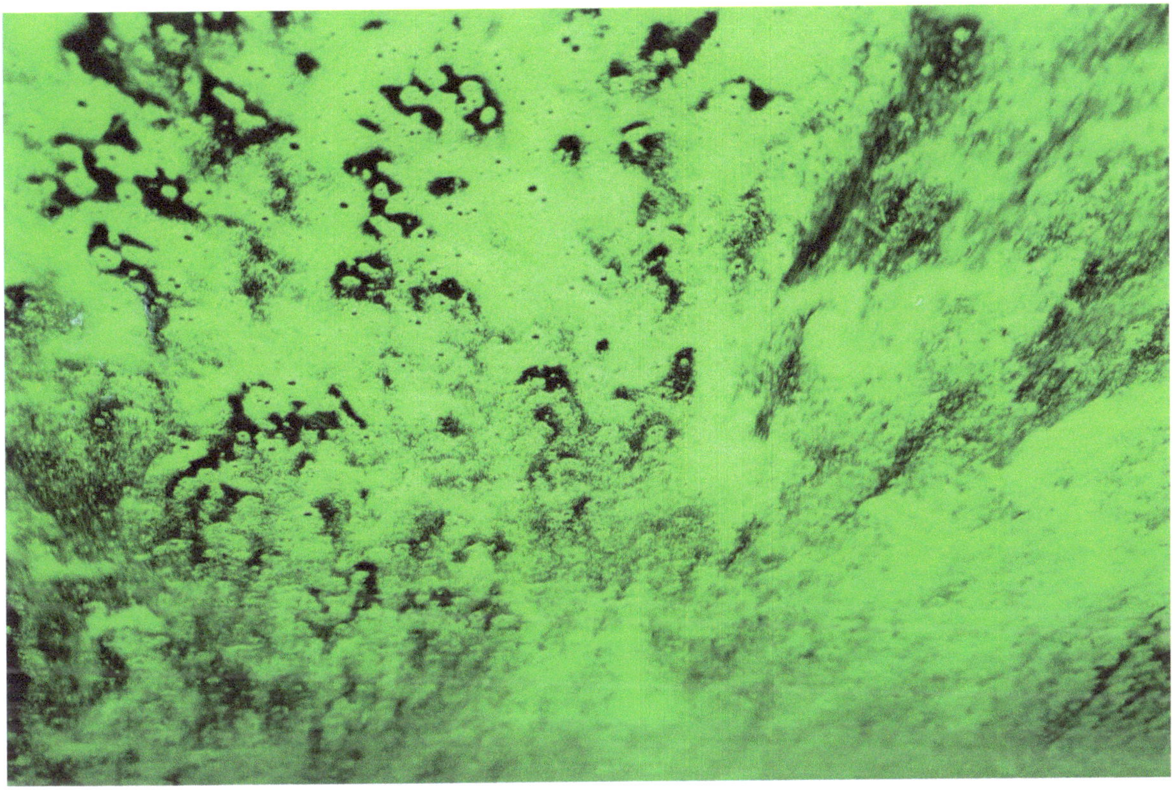

The Color of Success Washing In

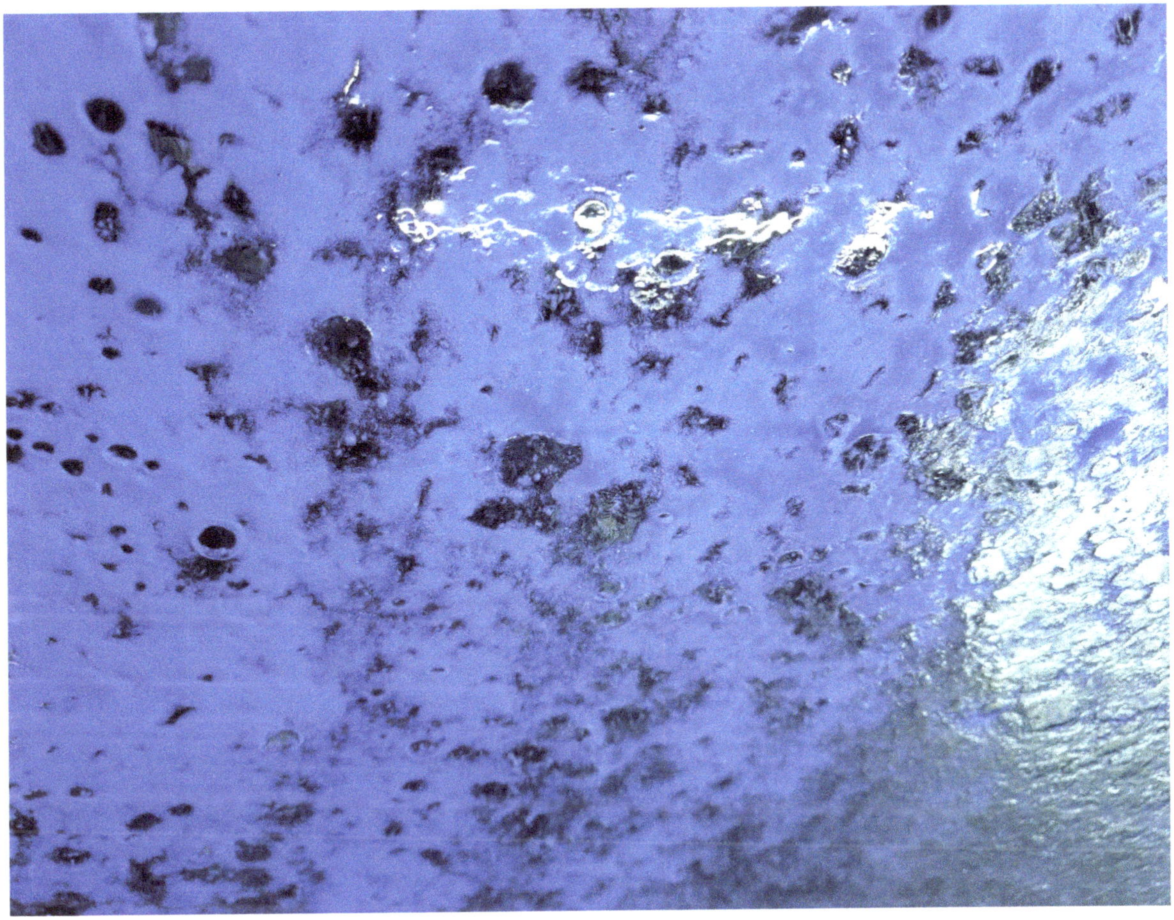

Basic Transparency

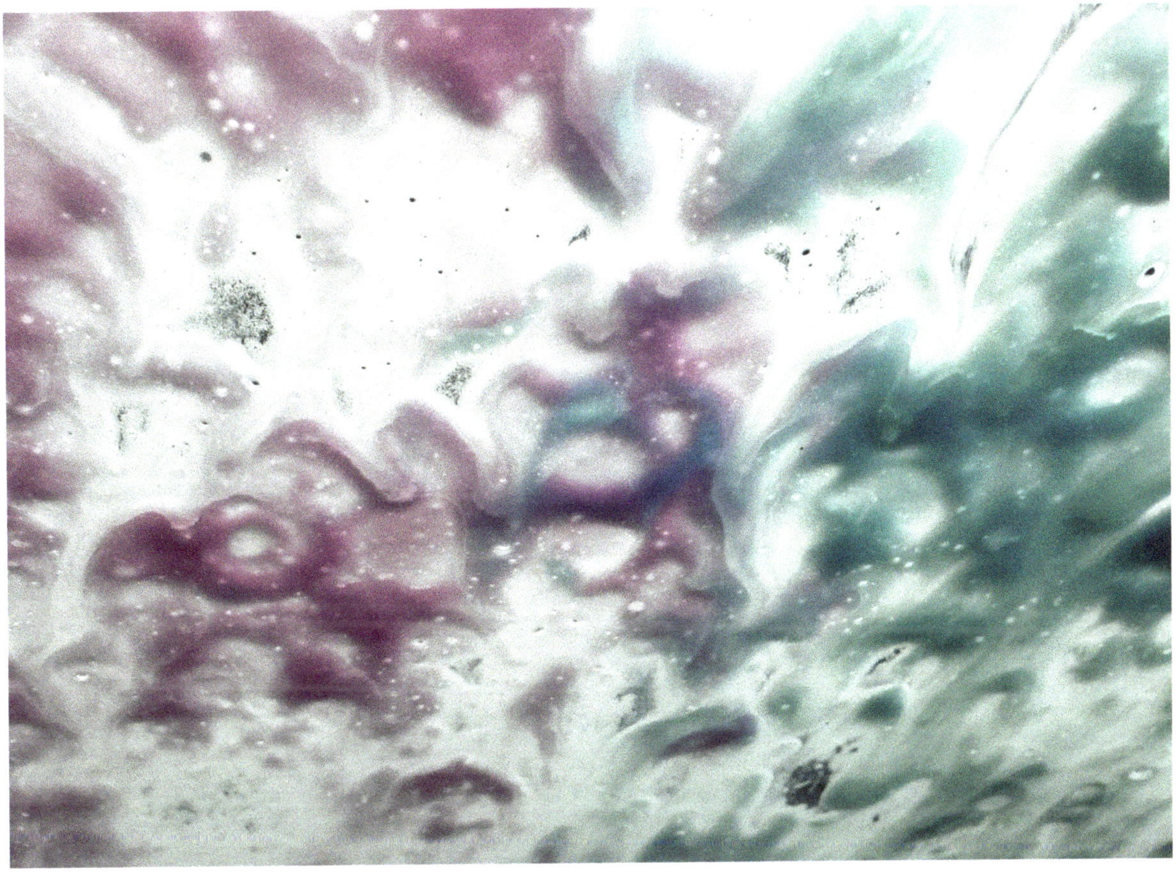

The Turn Coats

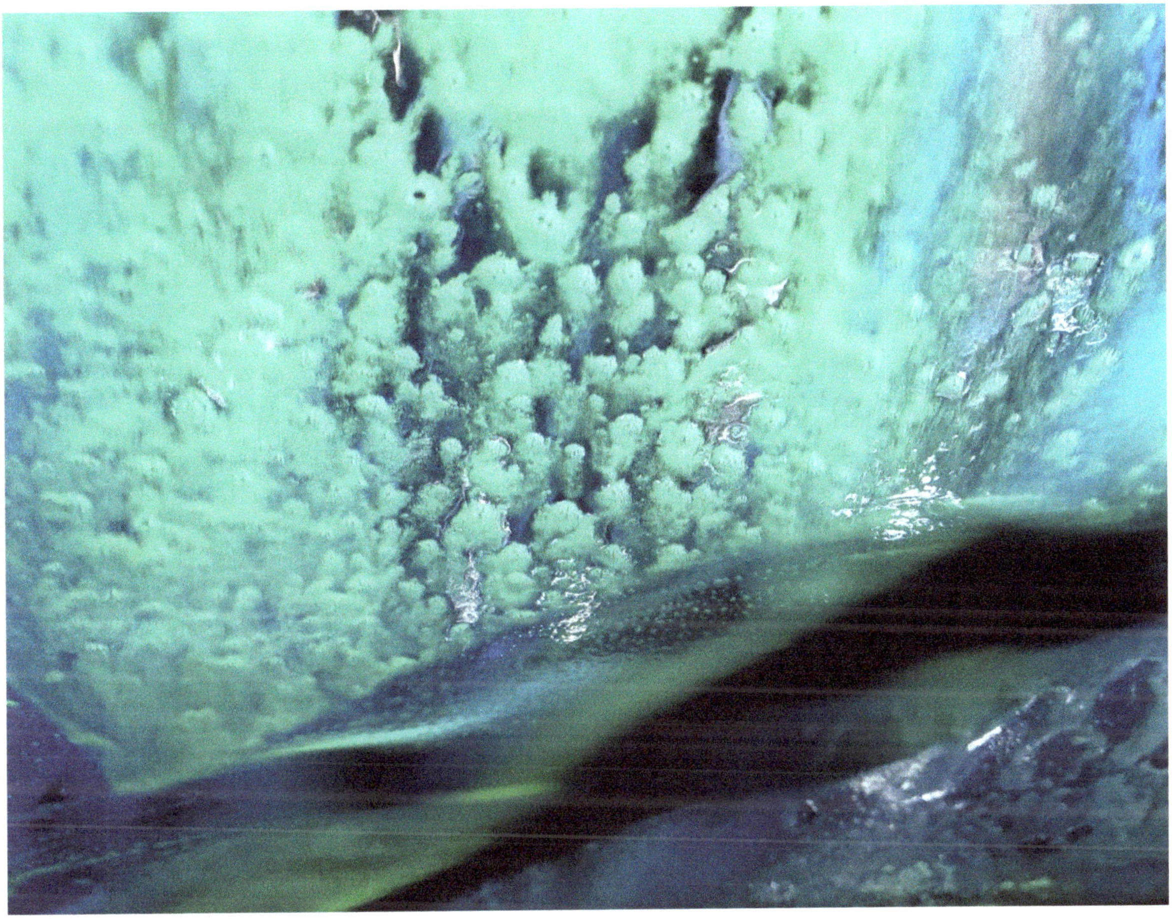

Complicated Romantic History

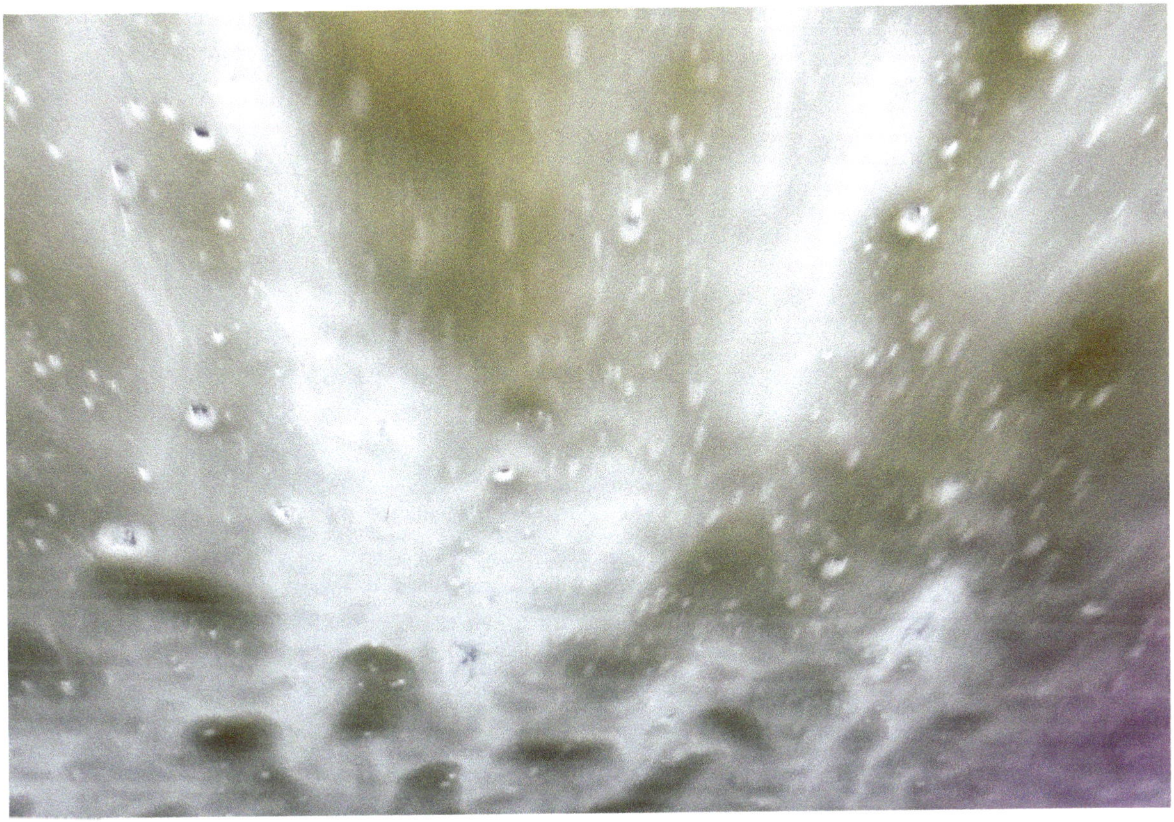

Brother's Widow, But They've Now Broken Up

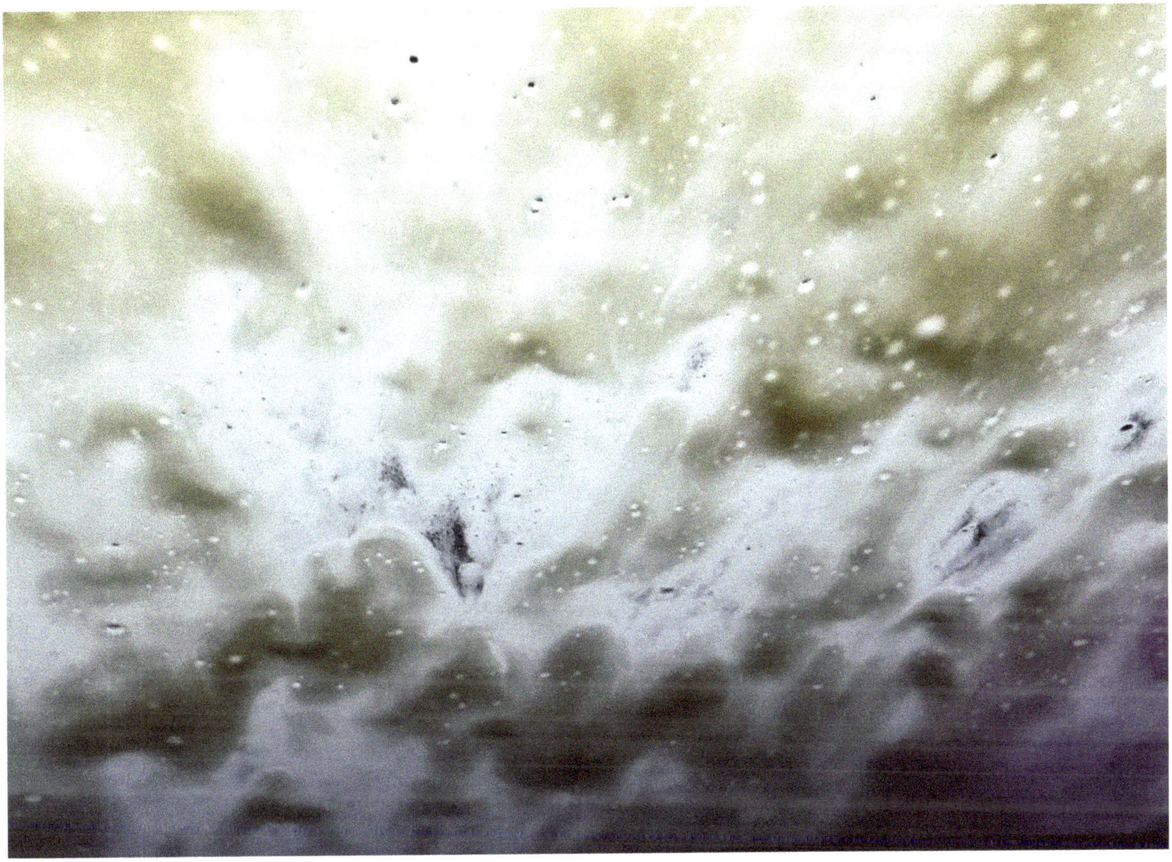

I Think I'm In Murky Waters

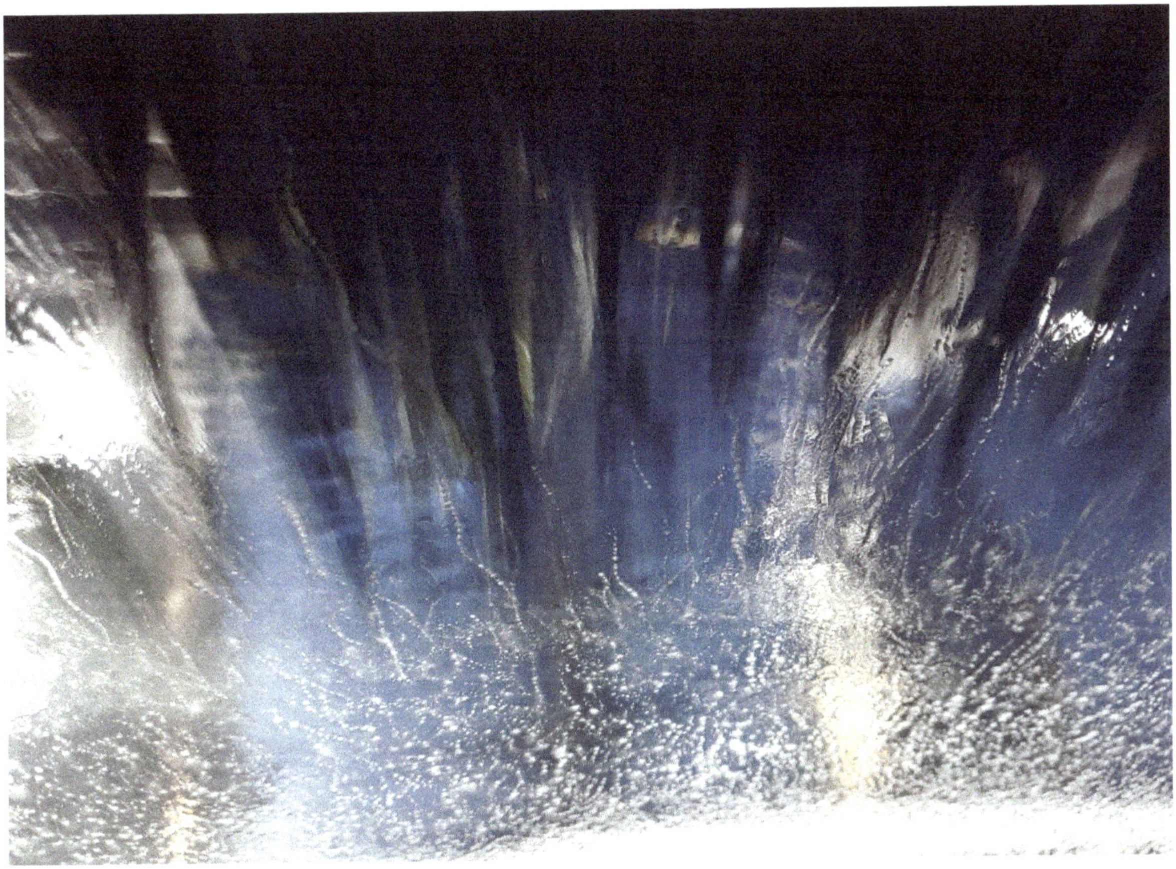

Paternity Suit

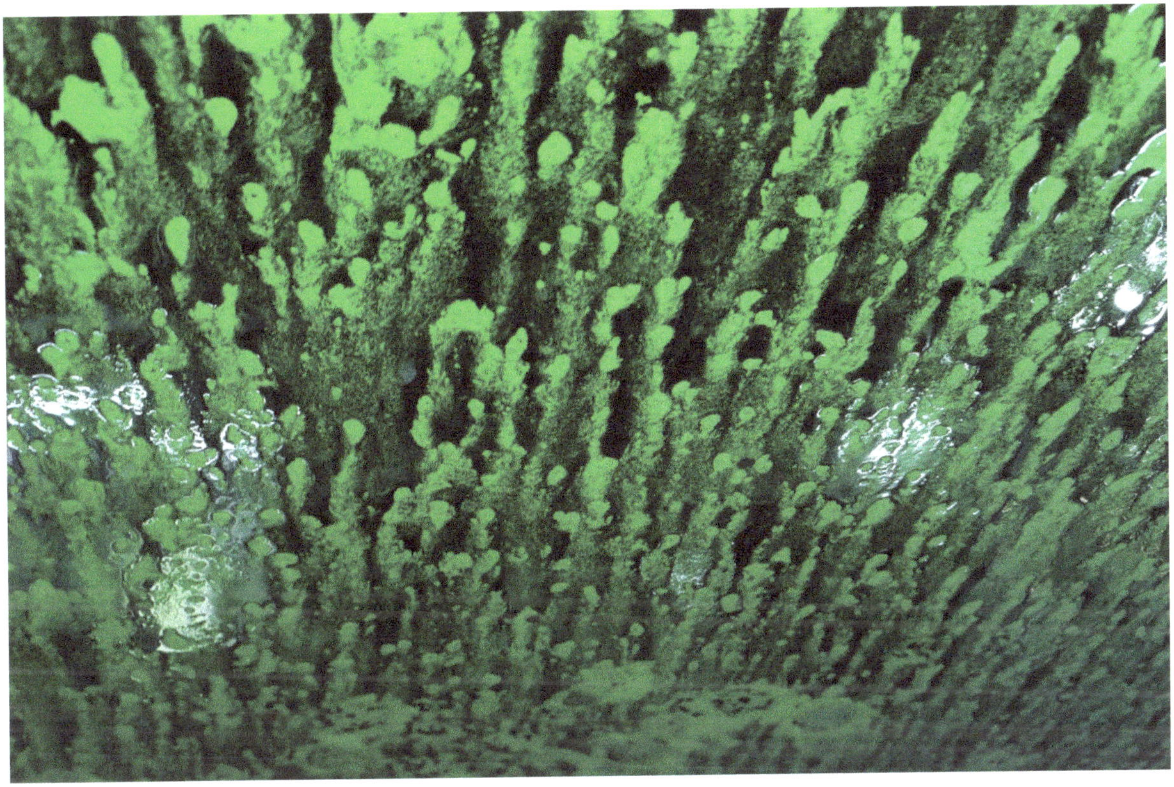

The Sign of the Beginning

Another Friday Night

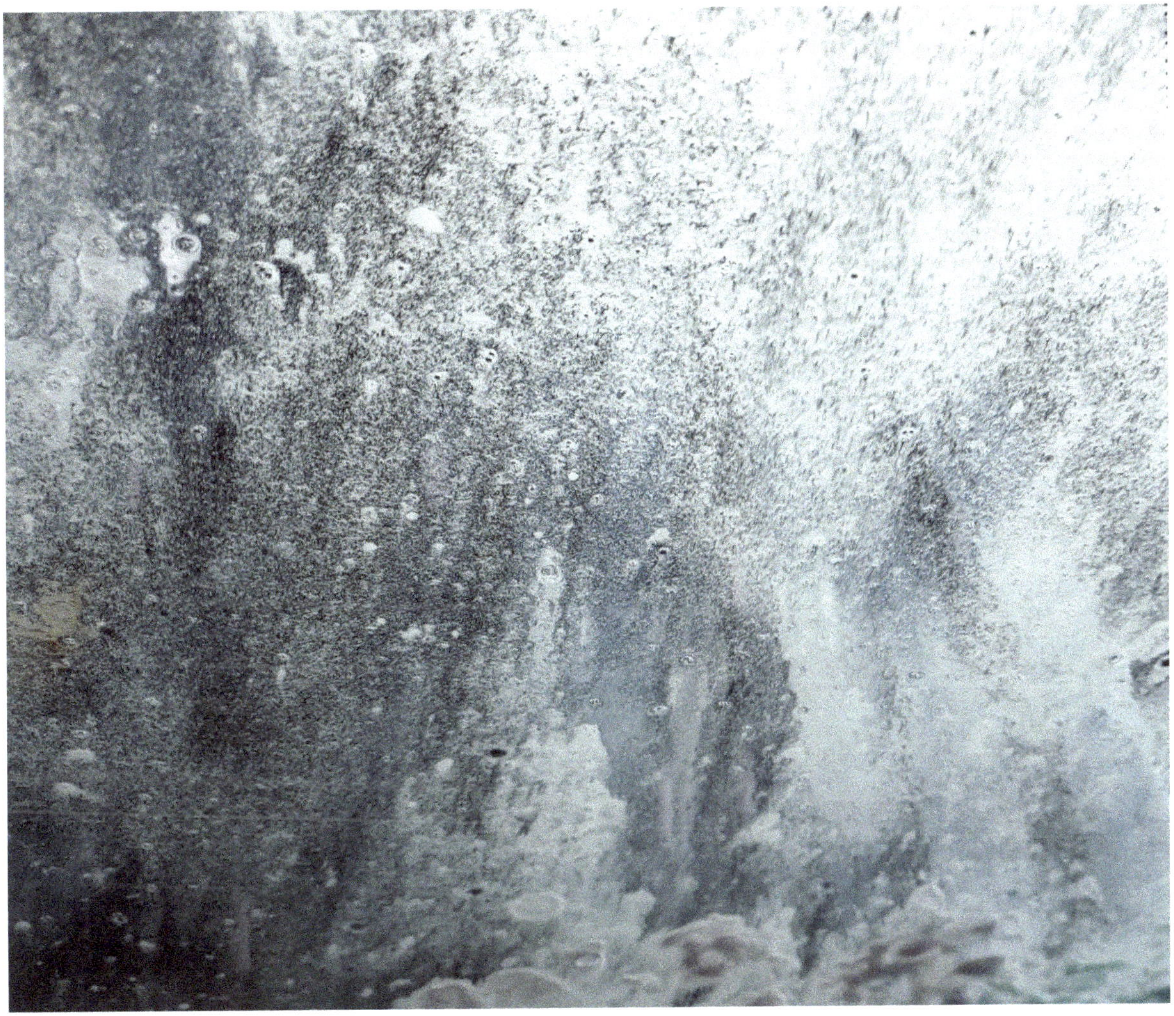

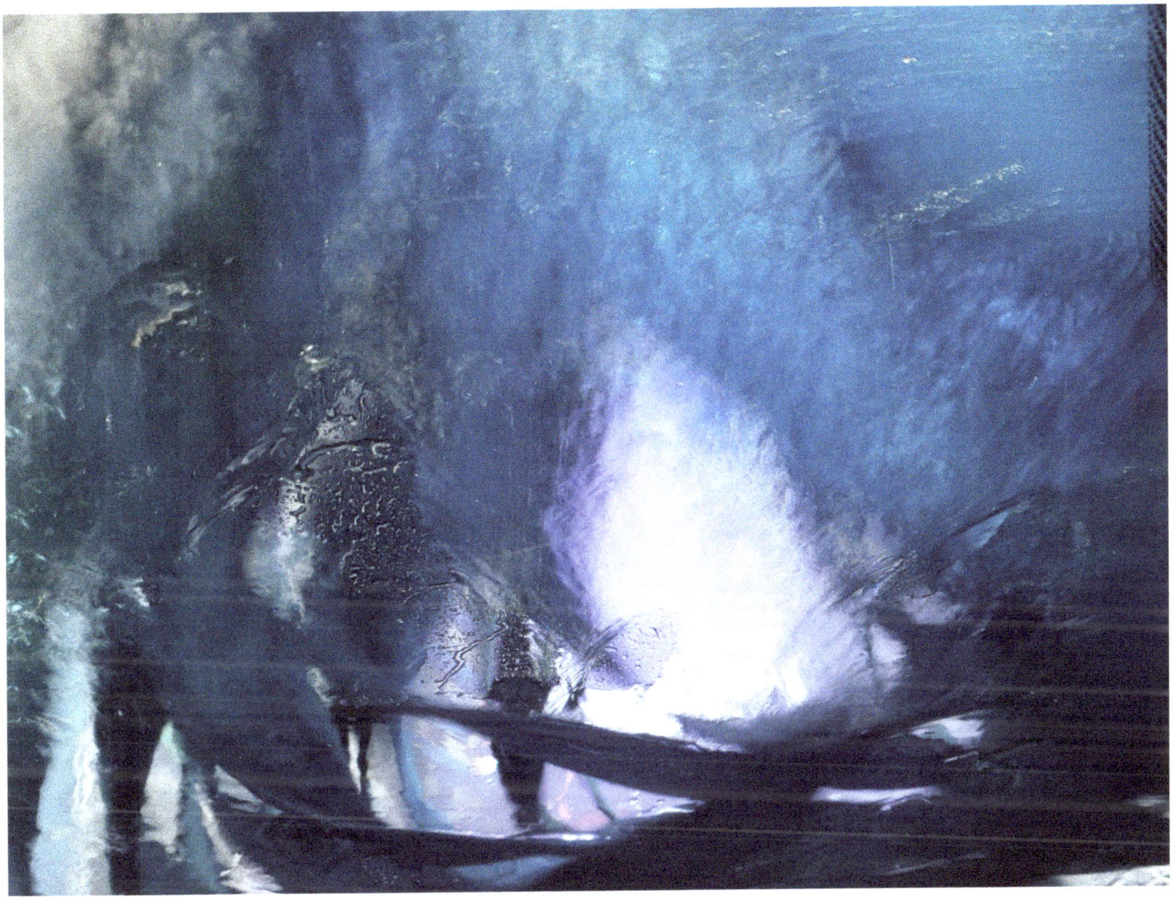

Swept Under by the Press

My Mind

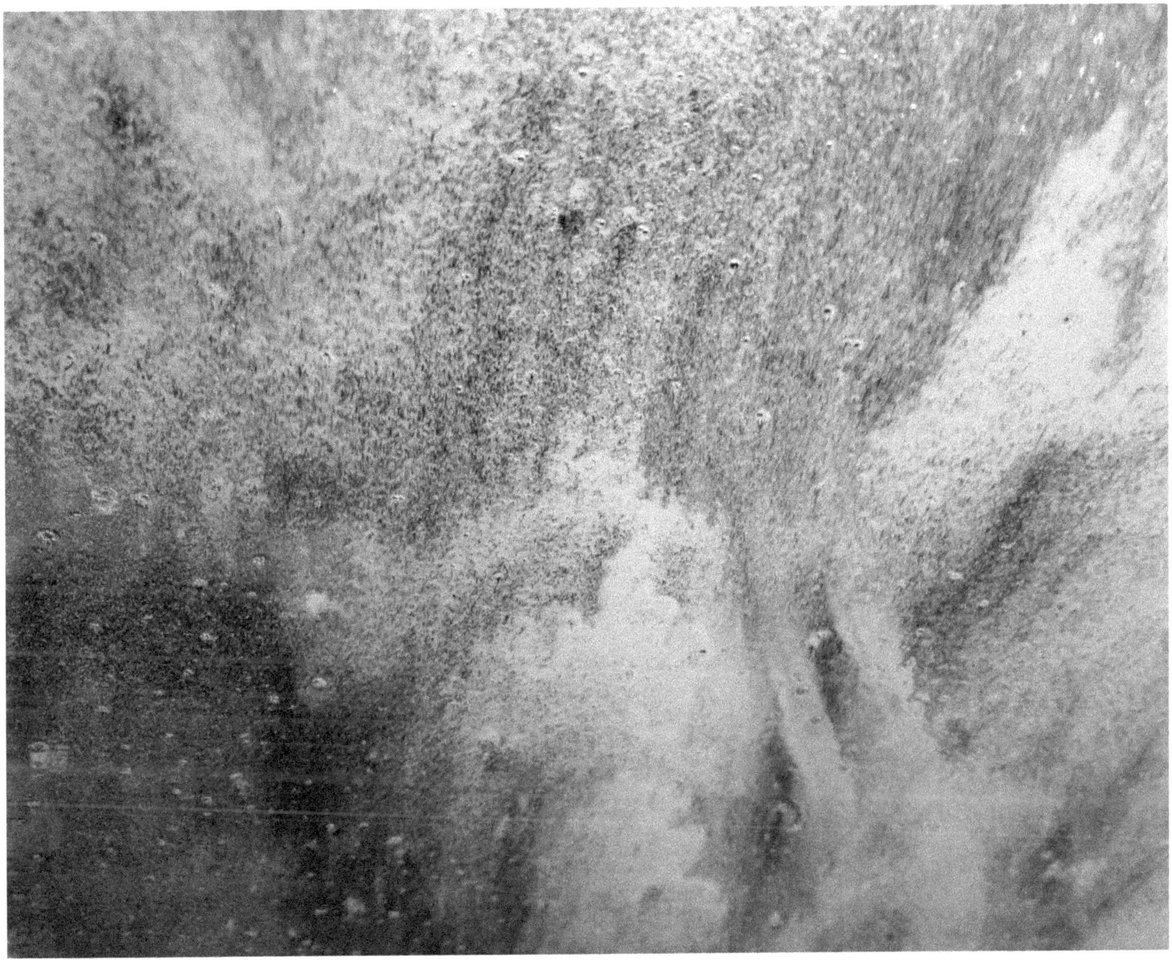

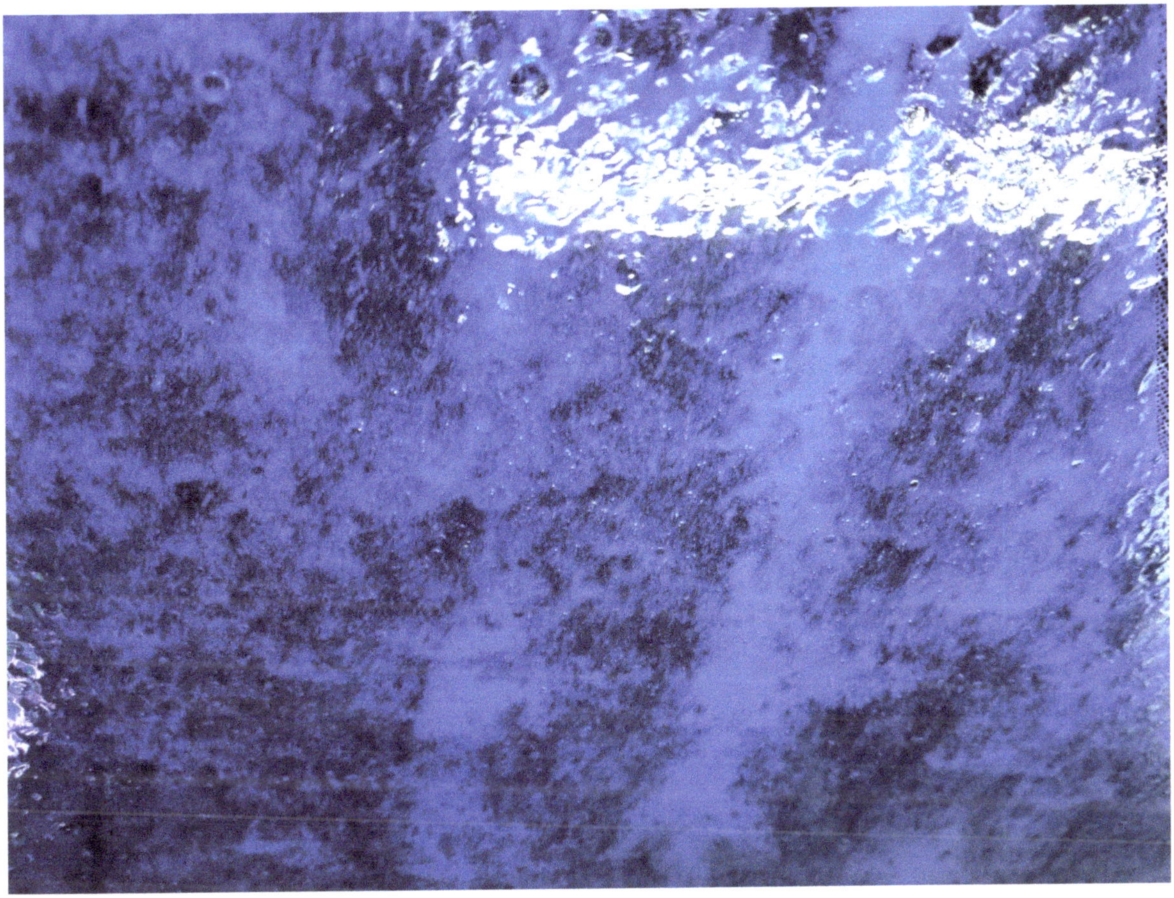

The Flight Back There with the Big Guy

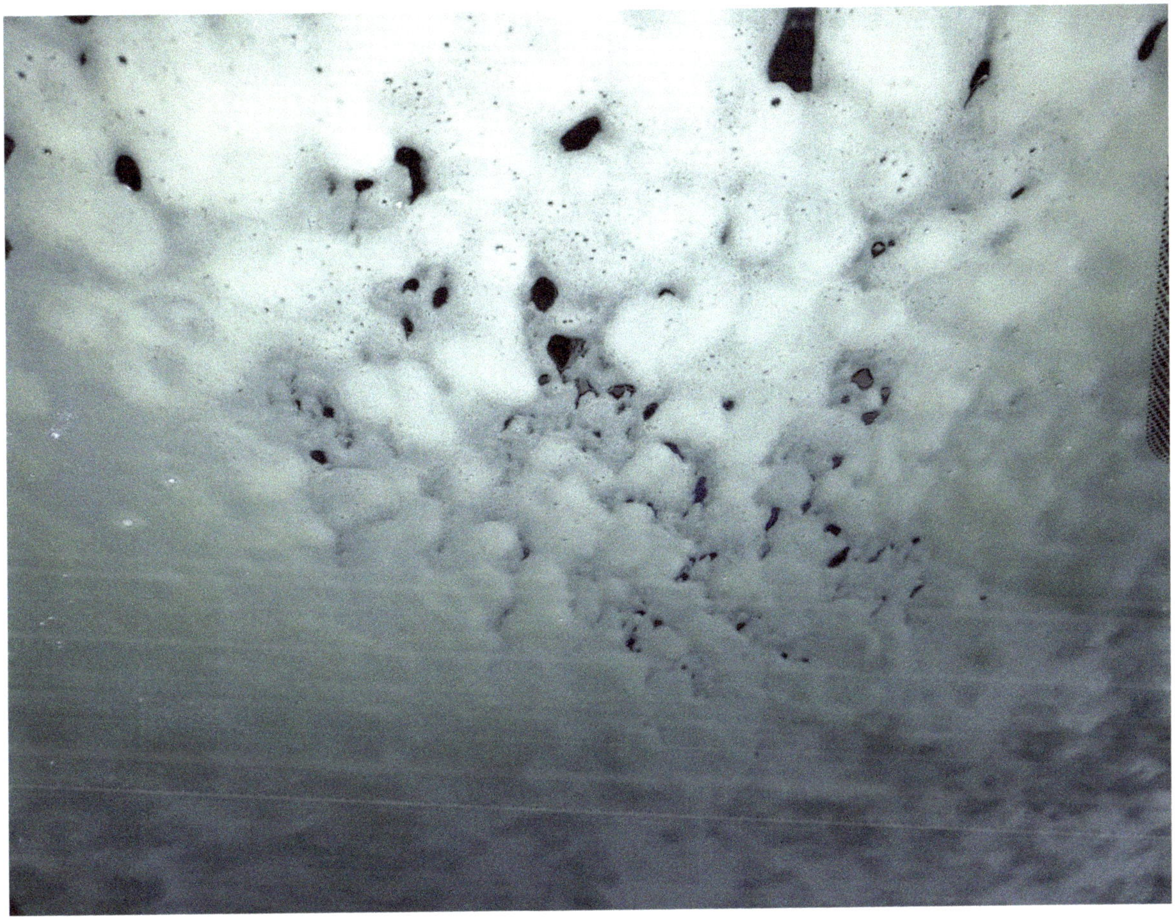

They Are Calling My Name

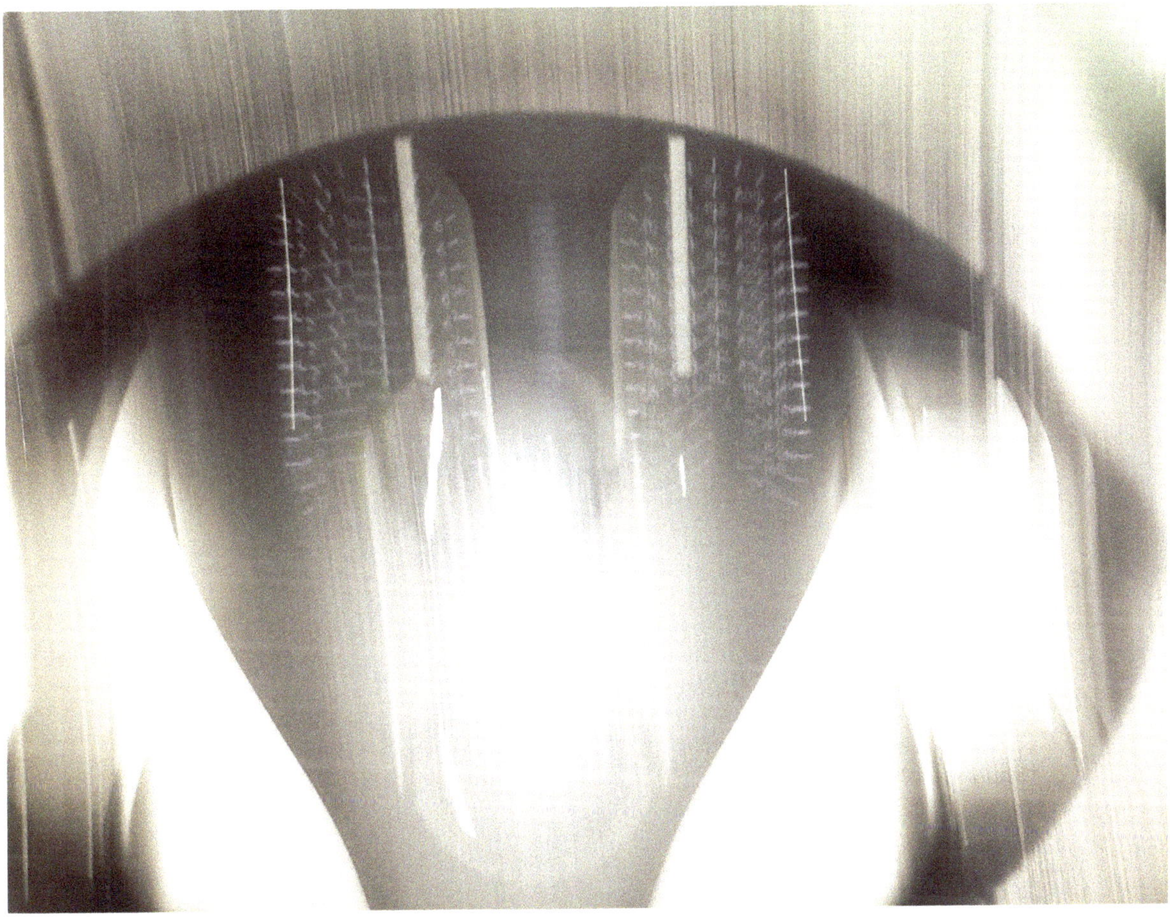

He's Watching Me

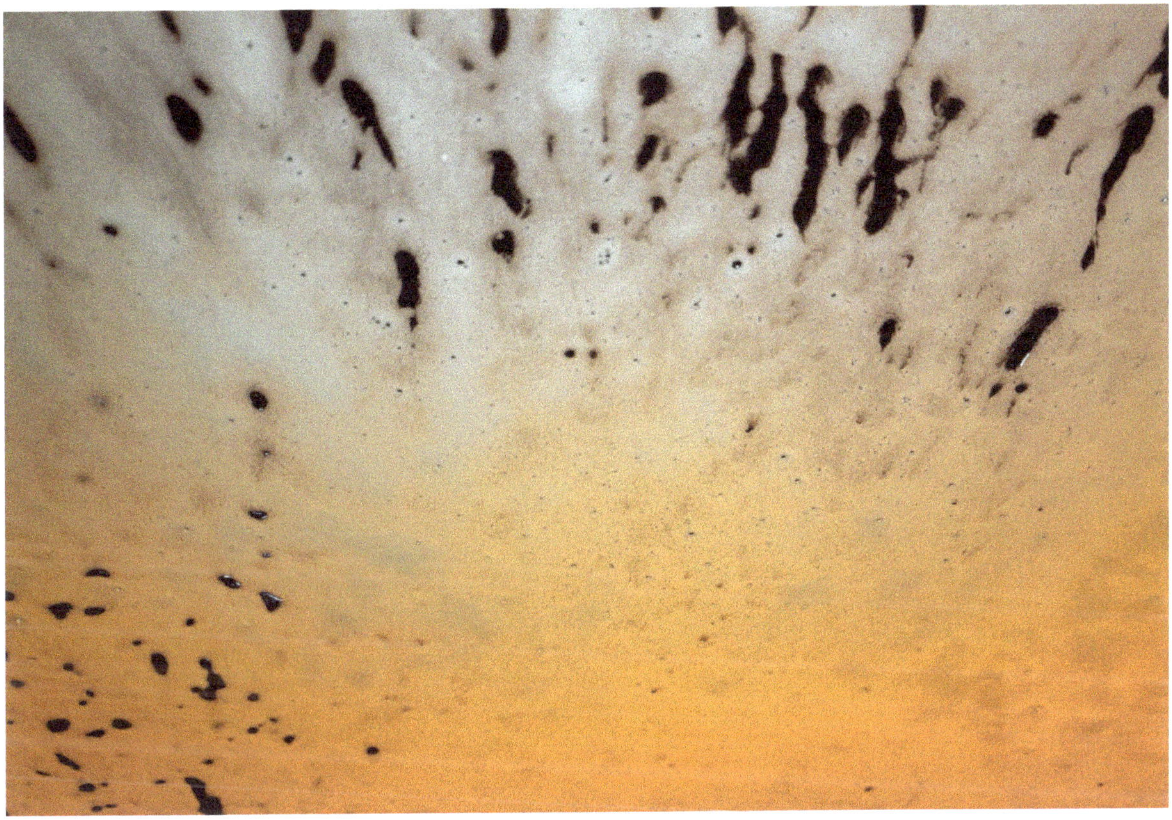

I See Red Are We Here Yet?

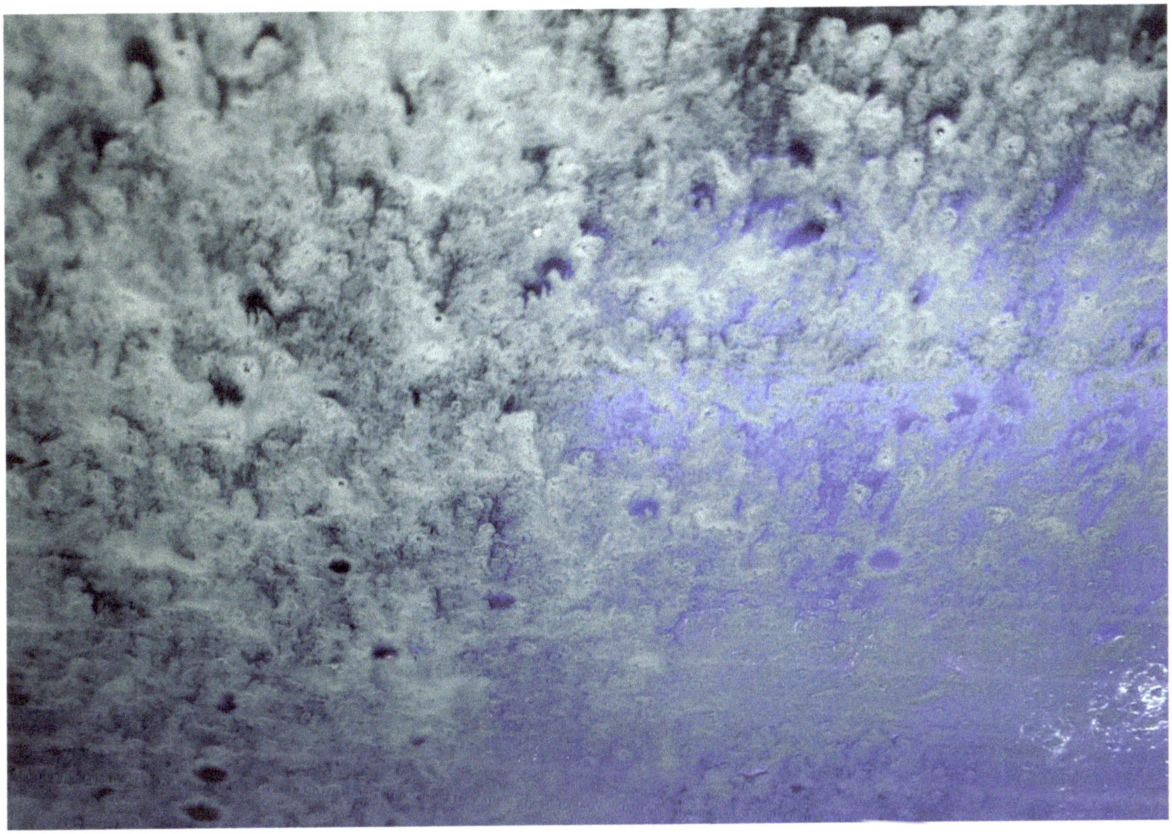

Life Is Good

www.ingramcontent.com/pod-product-compliance
Ingram Content Group UK Ltd.
Pitfield, Milton Keynes, MK11 3LW, UK
UKHW061950290726
14090UKWH00021B/1168

9 780578 351476